RAIN

Dark as Water in Winter

a play plus poems
Eileen Albrizio

ACKNOWLEDGEMENTS

The Stealing of a Winter Heart
  Underwood Review, Fall/Winter 1999
Depression at my Door
  Common Ground Review, Fall/Winter 1999
Something for Florence
  Common Ground Review, Fall/ Winter 1999
Self-portrait
  Common Ground Review, Spring/Summer 2000

First Edition.

RAIN, DARK AS WATER IN WINTER

Photographs

Editors
Suzy Lamson and Connie Magnan-Albrizio

www.yeolde.org
yeolde@webcom.com

ISBN: 1-889289-53-1

Printed in the United States by:
Morris Publishing
3212 East Highway 30
Kearney, NE 68847
1-800-650-7888

for
Wayne
I love you
always
thank you for helping me find myself
and still
believing I'm beautiful

for
Connie, my mother
from your writing
I have been inspired to write

for
Fran, my father
thank you for
inspiring Connie to write

for
Victoria
thank you for your love of poetry

for
Artemis Rising
thank you for your eyes and insight

INTRODUCTION

In this, her second collection, Eileen Albrizio demonstrates even more forcefully her ability to use formal verse to create poems which reach out and pull us in with the beauty of their words and the immediacy of their emotion. Here there is no language wrenched to fit into a stilted pattern, no feeling damped by the weight of sclerotic form. The work speaks, and we gladly listen.

In *Rain*, the verse play in one act which begins the collection, she uses meter and rhyme so subtly that the reader can hardly identify the patterns on which it is based. Yet the effects sink in subliminally. These effects are a sense of music, and a sense of otherworldliness, a feeling that this ongoing conversation between the two characters, which at first seems so ordinary, is something very much out of the ordinary. As the dramatic tension builds, this element transforms itself into a feeling of eeriness and impending doom.

In the 36 pieces which comprise the "Dark as Water in Winter" section of the book, Albrizio seems to delight in the range of forms at her deft fingertips. In "Something for Florence," she uses the pantoum to evoke the repetitive, circular thought and speech patterns of the elderly. In a variety of sonnets, she sculpts strong emotions into figures both solid and flowing. The rhyme royale "Self-Portrait" gives us a poignant center, augmented and intensified by the contrasting lyrical frame which surrounds it. "Dancing in a Simple Paradise," a terza rima, is pure sensual delight.

And so it goes, from haiku to villanelle, through couplets, triolets, and kyrielle to forms of her own invention, Eileen Albrizio here shows us the range and depth of her skills, and they are impressive. This is a collection to read not once, but many times, to delight in and to let its power sink into our souls.

Linda Yuhas

TABLE OF CONTENTS

RAIN

a verse-play
in one act

CHARACTERS

RAIN, a single woman in her mid-thirties

PERFIDY, a single man in his mid-forties

The action takes place in Rain's bedroom. The time is the present.

RAIN
a verse-play in one act

(The curtain rises on a bedroom. The lights come up to dim revealing a bed center stage, made with intricately matching dark linens. The bed is angled out slightly, so it is fully visible to the audience. Stage left of the bed is a nightstand. A small light, alarm clock and glass of water rests on top. Upstage right of the bed is a bookshelf overflowing with books. An oversized window, dressed in sheers, rests on the stage right wall. The stage right wall is angled out so the window itself is in full view of the entire audience. The bedroom door is on the upstage wall left of the nightstand. The lights remain low, giving the illusion of night. A figure moves restlessly in the bed. Rain, a woman in her mid-thirties, bolts upright in bed letting out a yelp. She reaches over and turns on the bed lamp. The lights come up a bit. She reaches for the glass and takes a sip of water.)

RAIN: Every time the night falls demons start to form, and when I close my eyes they fill my sleep. They multiply in number then begin to swarm, invading the memories I keep. *(She pulls the covers aside, and rises from the bed. She is wearing simple bedclothes, perhaps a tee shirt and a pair of shorts. She crosses to the window.)* I pray they fade with daylight but they're sneaky creatures, tip-toeing in my thoughts throughout the day. *(She pushes open the sheers. An early morning gray enters the room.)* As the light drops on their faces I recognize their features, and know too well forever they will stay inside my mind, inside my heart, their blood flows through each vein. Burning, stinging tears flood my eyes. One travels down my cheek like hot Brazilian rain. It hits the ground but it never dies. *(She crosses back to the stage left side of the bed and sits.)* It dissipates, turns to mist, settles on my skin...slowly works its way into my pores. Instinctively it starts the journey once again to terrorize the one that it

5

adores. *(She rests her head back on the pillow. The lights fade to black. The room remains dark except for a spotlight which comes up on Perfidy, a man in his early to mid forties, standing down right. He is neatly, but casually dressed.)*

PERFIDY: Desire flows from my tongue in words well rehearsed. Lands softly on her lips and in her lap. Worms its way inside, words and meaning reversed. Instantly she falls into my trap. *(Only Perfidy can be seen as he crosses to the bed and revels in the sheets. Rain is not there.)* Ravenous, greedy, I swallow up her purity. Careful not to harm what I invest. And in the moment I am sure of my security, I back away letting it digest. *(Throws back the sheets and rises from the bed.)* I feel my stomach acids eat away her virtue. The glow around her face turns to gray. Repelled by the one with passion I pursue, I can only push aside and turn away. *(Crosses down right, the spotlight follows.)* Revulsion builds inside me. I rise without a word. Her empty carcass sinks into the bed. And as I close the door I'm feeling quite absurd. Yet, go along, leaving her for dead. But I'll return. With time gone by she'll overlook my malice. I'll come prepared to take from her again. And once more with avarice I'll drink from her chalice, and she will never know where I have been. *(The spotlight fades to black. The lights come up to dim revealing Rain sitting on the down left edge of the bed. She wears a terry-cloth robe, and is rubbing her hair with a towel. Her legs and feet are bare. Perfidy stands motionless in the dim light. She does not acknowledge he is there.)*

RAIN: I try to wash him from my skin. His residue remains. He's present in my every humble task. *(She strokes her legs with the towel.)* He's in my mind...my heart...my blood. He courses through my veins. My need for him impossible to mask. *(The spotlight appears on Perfidy down right. It is as if he is not actually in the room. Rain does not react to his appearance as if she expected him* *there in her mind. He stands down right, motionless, watching her.)* His shadow looms above me. Watching every move. Deliberately I step through every hour. Believing he is watching, yet hoping I can prove I have worth, that without him I have power. *(She crosses down right and stands outside his spotlight. Perfidy stands motionless watching her.)* But even when I know he's miles and miles away I work as if he's hanging overhead. And when I see him next he is ignorant, I pray. He doesn't see the wounds that I have bled. *(She walks the circumference of the spotlight surrounding Perfidy without stepping over the boundary of light and dark.)* Perfidy. You punish me. You chain me with your treachery. You bind my will, shackle my abandon. *(She crosses to the door, opens it as if to leave, then shuts it hard without leaving.)* Perfidy. You punish me, filling me with lechery. I succumb to all that you demand. In time my strength falls from my bones, sinks into the earth. The soil provides no food for it to grow. It rots instead and I am left empty, without worth. My merit lies in what you will bestow. Dormant, the demons sleep. But soon they will arise, tend to their task of driving me insane. The only way to keep from being crushed under their lies is to hear you calling out my name. *(She crosses to the bed and lies down. She remains motionless in the bed.)*

PERFIDY: Rain. *(The spotlight disappears. The lights fade to black. A moment later, the lights come up to full. Rain is standing by the window facing out. Perfidy is standing by the door facing Rain. Her back is to him. He has his hand on the doorknob, closing the door behind him as if he has just entered. Rain is now dressed, but still her feet are bare.)* Good morning, Rain.

RAIN: *(She turns to him. A smile on her face.)* Perfidy!

PERFIDY: *(Crossing to her)* Looking out for me?

RAIN: *(Embarrassed)* Oh, no. Just admiring the view.

7

PERFIDY: *(Embracing her)* And I as well. For it's you I've come to see. In the time I was away I thought of you. Last night you walked through my dreams, brushed against my skin. Your face was blank, expressionless and hollow. I beckoned your embrace. My blood surged within. You kept on walking and I couldn't follow. What does it mean?

RAIN: I do not know.

PERFIDY: Where were you going, Rain?

RAIN: It was your dream, not mine. I wasn't there. If you ask me the dream itself was really quite inane. There isn't any cause for your despair. *(Perfidy crosses to the bed and sits. She remains at the window.)*

PERFIDY: You didn't want me. That I know. You ignored my pleas. With every step my hunger for you grew. You left me Rain, without a care, begging on my knees. You never spoke, but deep inside I knew. You didn't want me.

RAIN: You don't know.

PERFIDY: Do you want me now?

RAIN: You're basing all your fears upon your dreams.

PERFIDY: Dreams are said to help us solve our waking plights somehow.

RAIN: Perhaps your plight isn't what it seems. *(Rain turns her back to him and looks out the window. Perfidy rises and crosses away from her down left.)*

PERFIDY: Perhaps not. Perhaps I wanted you to walk away, for I desire what I cannot own. And with your body turned from me, indifference you display, I need you more

8

than I have ever known. *(Rain straightens, turns her head slightly with interest but keeps her back to Perfidy. Perfidy crosses to Rain and stands behind her.)*

RAIN: You need...

PERFIDY: *(Speaking close enough for his breath to be felt in her ear but not touching her)* Your skin...your breath...your voice singing in my ear. Your heart beat pounding close against my chest. Your sweat...your blood...your heart...your mind. All that you hold dear. All that you desire to be caressed.

RAIN: You do not know what I desire.

PERFIDY: I know more than you think. I know all about what travels through your head. You act aloof, uncaring, yet you're really on the brink of swallowing every word I've said. You accumulate every phrase, store them in your mind. Use them as a blanket when I'm gone. They'll warm your heart and ease your soul when the world's unkind. Keep you cozy at the break of dawn. *(Rain turns to face Perfidy. He grabs her shoulders.)* I know more than you think dear Rain. I know what's in your heart. Thoughts of me set the beat in motion. I know more than you think even when we are apart. Each step you make is based in pure emotion. *(He pauses slightly.)* You're shivering.

RAIN: *(Breaking his grip, she crosses down right.)* No, I'm not.

PERFIDY: I'm certain that you were. I'm sure I felt you tremble in my palm.

RAIN: Just a chill. A breeze perhaps.

PERFIDY: Perhaps it was a purr.

RAIN: No, a chill.

PERFIDY: But the air is calm. *(The curtains to the window flow with the push of air.)*

RAIN: There, you see. There is a breeze.

PERFIDY: *(Crossing down to her)* Oh, yes. I feel it now. *(He caresses her arms from behind her.)* As it tramples on your skin it leaves a trail. *(Rain crosses down center.)* Don't leave me, Rain.

RAIN: Perfidy.

PERFIDY: Before you, I avow my need for you. A need that will prevail despite your lack of interest, or what appears to be. Tell me, Rain. Why do I scare you so?

RAIN: Scare me?

PERFIDY: Yes. That's what I guess. You barely look at me. I'll leave. If you want me to I'll go. *(Perfidy begins to cross right to the door. Rain stops him before he can cross past her. They are both standing down center.)*

RAIN: No! Stay. I...need you here. I'm not scared...just confused. I need to feel your breath, to hear you speak. I don't want you to feel as if you've been abused. I'm not trying to be mean.

PERFIDY: You're just meek. *(Perfidy takes Rain in his arms and kisses her on the mouth. He embraces her so Rain is unable to see his face. He is smiling. The lights fade to black. A spotlight comes up on the bedroom door. The door is closing with the operator (Perfidy) on the outside, out of view of the audience. The door closes hard. The spotlight disappears and the lights come up to dim revealing Rain alone in the bed. She rises wearing*

10

nothing but a slip. She crosses to the window. The curtains to the window flow with the push of air. She rubs her arms.)

RAIN: He walks away so easily and in his wake the breeze tramples on my skin and leaves a trail. Once I gave myself to him he took from me with ease, absorbing all I am in great detail. Leaving me with nothing... *(She smells the palms of her hands.)* just the slightest scent. A memory at best of what has passed. I wonder if he's been here. *(She pushes apart the sheers in the window and looks out.)* I wonder where he went. I wonder why the rapture doesn't last. The moment he walks out the door the air turns sour and thick. My hands are soiled. My throat is filled with bile. The hope that I will hear from him fades with every tick. What remains is loathsome and vile. For what remains is me, patiently awaiting the demons that are destined arrive. Then they come, one by one, eagerly creating a place inside my mind where they can thrive. They eat away at my thoughts, replace them with their own. Artisans at forming my depression. They rip apart my sanity. Suck marrow from my bone, and Perfidy becomes my sole obsession. Familiar are the fiends. Repugnant is their comfort. They form so thick I swallow them like air. They beat me down and break me, but I don't attempt to thwart their strategy to glut me with despair. *(She crosses to the bed and lies down.)* I'll try to sleep, then time will pass, and all the day's events will be forgotten, at least for tonight. Perhaps my dreams will solve what my waking life prevents, giving me the answer to my plight. *(A spotlight shines on the bedroom window. Perfidy is peering in from the outside. His head and shoulders are visible. Rain is sleeping in the bed. Occasionally she tosses or turns.)*

PERFIDY: I love to watch her sleep, moving restlessly in bed. Aroused, she doesn't know that I'm around. I love to imagine what goes on inside her head. Careful not to make

11

a sound. Thrilled in her discomfort. Enraptured by her torment. Satisfied that I have caused her pain. It means I'm paramount if she continues to lament. And I'll make sure her grief will never wane. I wish you strained and tortured dreams while I invade your sleep with visions of what will never be. I will go when I am sure that I have seen you weep. Certain you are filled with Perfidy. *(Rain tosses and turns then bolts upright in bed. The spotlight remains on Perfidy.)*

RAIN: He watches me. I feel him. I hear him in my head. He guides the demons to each synapse. I can't escape you Perfidy. You're here to stay I dread, controlling me, ruling my collapse. Leave me please I beg of you. A moment of peace. An instant of relief from your domain. Tell me demons, will I feel this torture ever cease? *(She lays her head back on the pillow. She does not acknowledge Perfidy's physical presence.)*

PERFIDY: Not as long as it gives me pleasure, Rain. *(The spotlight disappears and Perfidy with it. Rain tosses a bit, then throws the covers back and rises from the bed. She shuffles through the bookshelf, finds a book, sits back on the bed and tries to read. She rises with the book in hand and paces back and forth. She flips a page, attempts to read while pacing, then flips the page back again. Turning the page back and forth she finally throws the book down on the bed in exasperation.)*

RAIN: I've read that phrase three times and I can't retain a word. It's imperative I find some diversion. I stare at the page and my vision becomes blurred. *(She crosses to the bookshelf and rummages through the books again.)* I must find an escape from this perversion. *(A sound comes from outside, like a trash can lid hitting the ground.)* What's that? Could it be him? It hasn't been that long. This doesn't keep with his usual routine. Has he altered his pattern? I hope that I'm not wrong, and can expect

12

less distance in between each encounter. Did he not get his fill? Perhaps he wants to pay me a surprise. I know he treats me like candy. Too much will make him ill. *(She crosses to the window and looks out, then turns back abruptly and beats her hands against her chest.)* Oh Rain, this is just what I despise. I've lost me. I'm nowhere. He's taken everything. Bit by bit, heart, mind and soul. He has complete possession. What started as a fling has left me an eternal black hole.

PERFIDY: *(From outside)* Rain!

RAIN: *(Crossing down center quickly, excited to hear Perfidy's voice. She stops suddenly.)* It's him! I don't want him. I don't want him here. I'm mercurial beyond my comprehension. He's at my door and I pray for him to disappear, for his existence engulfs the room in tension. But, I pine for him again the moment he is out of sight, as if the thought of him is somehow more appealing than the actual person. Oh, there is no delight in this relationship or what I am feeling

PERFIDY: *(Again from outside)* Rain!

RAIN: *(She runs to the bedroom door and locks it, then crosses to the bedside lamp and turns the switch. The lights fade to dim. She crosses to the front of the bed and crouches on the floor, her arms wrapped around her knees.)* The lights low. Silent. I'll pretend that I'm not in. Maybe then he'll just turn and walk away. It's hard to resist, like the devil tempting sin. I want to run to him and beg for him to stay.

PERFIDY: *(Closer)* Rain!

RAIN: I'll say I was in the shower and didn't hear him call. Better yet, I'll say I was out with friends. Perhaps he won't bother to mention it at all. But then I'll never know

13

what he intends for me tonight. He may just want to chat. That would be nice, if it were only so. He may not want to take me. I can't be sure of that.

PERFIDY: *(At the door shaking the door handle)* Rain!

RAIN: If I don't answer soon he'll go. *(She hesitates a moment, then rises. She rushes to the door and unlocks it. She throws the door open. Perfidy is on the other side with his back turned as if about to leave.)* Perfidy! *(He turns to her, walks slowly forward into the room with Rain stepping back in perfect synchronization.)* I was asleep. Forgive my hesitation. What a surprise! I didn't know it would be you.

PERFIDY: *(Annoyed)* You locked the door.

RAIN: *(Turning her face from him)* Oh, did I?

PERFIDY: A simple explanation. I deserve that much.

RAIN: Yes. I'm sure you do. I didn't know I'd locked the door. I was just so weary and you were the last one I expected. I've had such a busy day. But that's all so dreary. There is no need for you to feel rejected. What brings you by?

PERFIDY: Why you of course. Aren't you glad I'm here? *(He takes her shoulders in his hands and turns her to him, forcing her to face him.)*

RAIN: Certainly. You're everything to me. Is there something on your mind?

PERFIDY: Only you, my dear. You're in my eyes. You're everything I see. I need you, Rain. I haven't long. I'm sure you'll understand. Give me what I need and I'll be on my way.

14

RAIN: Perfidy. I'll gladly give you all that you demand. But I implore you find a way to stay.

PERFIDY: You mourn my absence with me here. Our visits are so brief. You mustn't waste this time with such projections. I hate to think that when I'm gone you're overcome with grief, or you think of what has passed with some objections. Each word we speak is eating up each precious moment past and there is no excitement on your face. I wish to bring you only joy and make each moment last in your memory, defying time and space. *(Perfidy begins to unbutton Rain's blouse. She looks away, helpless, then suddenly grabs his hands in hers as if to stop him.)* Why stop me? Don't tell me you are playing hard to get. That's very coy, but hardly apropos. Come now dear. Remove your blouse. Reciprocate and let me take you quickly for soon I must go.

RAIN: *(She continues to hold his hands tightly, restricting his movements. She avoids looking him in the eye.)* Do you love me?

PERFIDY: What?

RAIN: I ask...Do you love me? *(Perfidy hesitates almost annoyed.)* I need to know if love brings you here.

PERFIDY: Silly girl. Of course. I desire you immensely. I find your insecurity most queer.

RAIN: *(Looking at him)* You should know best of all desire and love are not the same. Love remains through every twist and turn. Desire needs oxygen to breath, feeding like a flame. Red hot at first but awfully quick to burn. Again...Do you love me? Will you call on me tomorrow if I don't give you what you want today? Will you judge my imperfections, scoff at my sorrow? Please. I need to know either way.

PERFIDY: *(Taking a deep breath. His voice hard)* I love you. If you sent me out I'd love you still. *(Rain loosens her grip and Perfidy walks away from her toward the door.)* It is pure love that brings me to you. It holds me by the hand and takes away my will. It governs everything I think and do. *(His hand on the door handle.)* Now if you're satisfied, is it best that I should leave? Or do you trust my words are sincere?

RAIN: *(Turning away so he can't hear her thoughts spoken out loud)* Oh Perfidy, I fear I don't know what to believe. I'm worried you are not as you appear. You have my heart. I must believe. I have no other choice. You're the only way that I can feel its beat. And though I would be satisfied to simply hear your voice, you must possess my soul to be complete. *(She turns back to him speaking for his ears.)* Your words fall before me and are clear to read. Premeditated, carefully laid out. They are sharp and I won't touch them for I would surely bleed, but I understand what they are about. Thoughts of me compel you to travel to my side. That should be enough for me to give you what you've come to take. For that I will abide by all you say and everything you do.

PERFIDY: *(Crossing to her, Perfidy wraps Rain in his arms tightly.)* Good girl. I knew you'd come around. Now precious time is wasted. I hunger for your touch to feel your skin. *(He kisses her hard on the neck.)* You whet my appetite and I like what I have tasted. *(He removes her blouse. She stands before him in a slip.)* It's time you open up and let me in. *(He picks her up, crosses to the bed, lays her down. As he sits beside her the lights fade to black. In the darkness the sound of a door opening and closing is heard. The lights come up to dim revealing Rain alone, motionless in the bed. A moment passes.)*

RAIN: Each time is quicker than the last. Each time less words spoken. Each time the end is the same. Carelessly he

16

takes from me leaving something broken, and I am the only one to blame. *(A spotlight comes up on Perfidy standing down stage right. Rain remains motionless in bed. She does not acknowledge he is there.)*

PERFIDY: She was hard to overcome. The antipathy was quick. My appetite laborious to sate. She demanded love but the thought made me sick. Still I'm satisfied with all that I ate. I need more time to build resistance in between each tryst. By then she will be eager to submit. When I arrive she will believe that she was greatly missed and won't require for me to admit my love for her before she relinquishes control of her will that I've worked hard to acquire. By next encounter I will own her heart, mind and soul. And I will supersede all desire. So I will stay away, far longer than before. At least that will be her belief. She won't suspect from time to time I'll listen at her door to ensure she is overcome with grief. Oh what a pleasing game this is, to always have the lead. She is so easy to manipulate, handing me her weakness, and hungrily I feed. How sweet it will be to make her wait. *(The lights fade to black. As the lights come up to dim we see Rain standing by the window staring out. The lights fade to black. A moment later, the lights come up to dim revealing Rain sitting on the bed, a pillow clutched to her face. She is sobbing. Perfidy appears in the window. He is smiling. The lights fade to black. As the lights come up to dim Rain is again standing by the window staring out. Perfidy is nowhere to be seen.)*

RAIN: I do not know how many nights have overcome the days. In the dusk I hope to recognize the outline of his body pushing through the haze. He's not there and I've come to despise the sparks of light that mock me as they dance on the brook, the barren trees that root in rocky ground, the crescent moon that slices the sky as I look into the night where no sign of him is found. *(The lights fade to black. As the lights come up to dim we see Rain standing upleft in front of the door with her back leaning*

17

against it.) Waiting, walking every inch of this room, which has become my entire universe. Withering, wandering about in the gloom with the demons who refuse to disperse. Ignoring my entreaties, my screams and my pleading. I've battled each and every one. Fatigued and alone, I try to stop the bleeding unaware a new day has begun. *(The lights fade to black. As the lights come up to dim, we see Rain sitting on the edge of the bed down center.)* I'm a prisoner of war of which I've created. Verities and falsehoods rage through my intellect. When verity succeeds in squashing all I have hated I am able to discern and dissect what is true and what is not. It's surprisingly transparent. This time alone allows a clearer vision. Though painful to understand, a truth now so apparent, I can...almost... come to a decision. *(The lights fade to black. The lights come up to dim with Rain standing by the window looking out. A sweater is carelessly tossed on the edge of the bed.)* The weeks passed are impossible to count and any ray of hope has turned to black. But there is...comfort with the dread that is beginning to mount as I realize he isn't coming back. *(Rain rises, puts on the sweater, briefly scans the room then exits. A spotlight appears on Perfidy who is standing outside the bedroom window looking in.)*

PERFIDY: She isn't here. How curious. The demons of her sleep have always lingered long past this hour. For her to wake before the first gray of dawn should creep is peculiar and leaves a taste that's sour in the back of my throat, and the doubt upon my brain dances in a black cloud of smoke. Why aren't you here waiting? Where have you gone to, Rain? What a suspicious dance you provoke. I will travel through the streets to find a glimpse of you, and again watch you from afar. Only then will this cloud vanish from my mind. Only then when I discover where you are. *(Perfidy ducks out of view. The spotlight vanishes. The lights come to full as Rain enters the room carrying a newspaper. She sits at the down left edge of the bed and opens the paper, folding back a page.)*

18

RAIN: Sleep didn't come to me last night, forced out of reach by tortured thoughts forward on my brain. The demons loomed in corners but were unable to breach my mind or interfere with my pain. Anguished as they were, my thoughts were bold and clear, for the first time of my own discretion. Absent were the shadows that clouded me with fear, forcing my thoughts to change direction. *(She rises and crosses to the window and looks out.)* As the horizon stretches with the birth of the day unanswered are the questions of the night. But a small amount of peace has come with Perfidy away... *(She pushes open the sheers. The gray of dawn enters the room.)* ...and for once I look forward to the light. *(She crosses back to the bed and opens the paper. She reads silently. Suddenly Perfidy bursts through the bedroom door. He is frenzied and out of breath. Rain, startled by Perfidy's entrance, rises hastily and stands by the window with the bed between them.)* Goodness! After all this time! Forgive my alarm. You've caught me off-guard, I'm afraid. Of course, I'm glad to see you. I don't mean any harm. Where have you been?

PERFIDY: It doesn't matter where I've stayed! You're here. I thought you would be out.

RAIN: Why would I be out?

PERFIDY: *(Attempting to regain his composure)* You didn't answer when I knocked.

RAIN: Strange. I've been here all along. Did you give a shout? Or try the door, I'm sure it was unlocked.

PERFIDY: I didn't want to wake you should you be sleeping. It was early, the dawn had yet to break.

RAIN: There's a change. That never stopped you before from keeping my company. Besides, I was awake.

19

PERFIDY: What could you have to do before the sun should rise that would take you away from your home?

RAIN: I tell you I was here and it's futile to disguise your desire to know where I roam. What difference does it make even if I was away? I had no warning you were calling.

PERFIDY: *(As if catching her at some wrong doing)* There! You see. I hear it in the words you say. Now out with it. The truth. No more stalling.

RAIN: Heavens, Perfidy. I have no reason to lie. I can't imagine what it is you wish to learn. What did you do, wait outside my window and spy on my every move, then wait for my return just to put me through this interrogation.

PERFIDY: So you were here.

RAIN: Yes.

PERFIDY: That makes no sense.

RAIN: What do you mean it makes no sense? What justification am I forced to invent in my defense? *(She tosses the newspaper on the bed and crosses to the window.)*

PERFIDY: That I've come back at all is amazing in itself, for as of late you offer very little. I'm constantly on trial defending myself, and with you as the jury, no acquittal can be expected, only condemnation. No one else would put up with such maligning Your dearth of respect and your callous denigration. Not to say your lack of looks and constant whining. I hardly believe there are any other men...or women if you will...who find you pleasing.

RAIN: *(Taking his words to heart, she submits slightly)* You are the only one. I can't remember when there was anybody else. You're most appeasing. But there are many contradictions. You are often most confusing. Sometimes your words resound with passion, but then you push me off as if you find my love amusing, and the love you have doled out I'm forced to ration.

PERFIDY: *(Crossing to the door)* I can't stand this bickering or the way you carry on. I have appointments and I'm already late.

RAIN: Before you leave, tell me why you came before the dawn and why you barged into my home in such a state.

PERFIDY: *(Hesitates for just a moment)* I came to share your bed ...to feel you breath while you slept. Long before you opened up your eyes I wanted to hear the soft moans as they crept from your dreams through your lips in gentle sighs. But, it's too late for that.

RAIN: *(Weak, but determined)* I'm not sure I understand. Is this equivocation of a sort? You say to come while I was sleeping was part of what you'd planned, yet my sleeping is what forced you to abort your scheme.

PERFIDY: You hurt me, Rain with all that you allude. I leave you to believe what you will. Only when your irrational behavior has subdued will I return. Although I want you still I can't have you now for the time has run out.

RAIN: Forgive me. My questions were unjust.

PERFIDY: Yes they were. You surely had no reason to doubt my intentions. I have appointments, now I must be on my way.

RAIN: I wish you didn't have to leave.

21

PERFIDY: We can't always have what we desire. I wish you hadn't thought that my goal was to deceive. I wish you hadn't thought of me a liar. *(He exits. Rain crosses to the door. She touches it but doesn't open it.)*

RAIN: The apology surprised me as it tripped from my tongue. It was habitual but lacking of veracity. It carried the tune of a song often sung but was unable to possess the capacity to reach beneath why he was here and what was said and uncover the truth of his intentions. Did he really want to share my dreams and share my bed, or were his words merely clever inventions? *(She crosses to the window and looks out as if to find Perfidy.)* When he threatened to go I prayed he would remain. I longed to feel the heat rise from his skin. I longed to taste his sweat as it fell like salty rain. I longed for him to take me from within. And now he's disappeared. My fate should be the same, left empty, in a solitary hell. *(She touches her face lightly.)* But today I remain more than just a frame. And in his absence I am able to quell the cries of the demons as they form outside my mind. Though it exists, the hunger is faint. And the barbed vines that usually bind my heart have stayed away without complaint. *(She looks to the bed, crosses to the bed, picks up the newspaper and sits comfortably. She opens the paper and begins to read.)* I am able to lift the words from the page and retain the story that they make. How comforting, to be able to engage in normality with nothing at stake. Still something knocks at the tip of my spine, a thought, plaguing and directed. Unwanted and alone in a world that isn't mine, I am convinced I will never be connected to anyone or anything. Forever outcast. He was right. His words are absolute. Through the lies and deception, from the first to the last, he speaks a truth that I can not refute. *(The lights fade to black. A spotlight shines on Perfidy standing down right.)*

PERFIDY: I was careless to face her without logic in my grip. I was foolish to stay away so long. She questioned my intent and watched for me to trip on my words to decipher what was wrong. Though her apology and her desire for me to stay proves I still control her will and own her heart. I must now frequent her bed to ensure she doesn't stray. I will limit the time we are apart. *(The spotlight follows Perfidy as he crosses to outside the window. The lights come up to dim with the spotlight still focused on Perfidy. He watches Rain as she lies on the bed reading.)* As she reads the words will lay heavy on her eyes and the world will disappear under its weight. As she sleeps in her dreams a new world will arise. There I can safely seal her fate. *(Rain lets the paper fall into her lap as she drifts off to sleep. The spotlight disappears and so does Perfidy. He reappears through the bedroom door and slips beside Rain in her bed. Rain tosses restlessly then bolts upright with a start. The lights come up to full. Perfidy, beside her, strokes her hair gently.)* You wake with such alarm. Your sleep brings no repose. When I'm away I fear you cannot rest. It's deceiving how peaceful you appear as you doze. That you were anxious I never would have guessed .

RAIN: I could feel someone beside me. Somehow I was aware of an intruder, a fear I couldn't shake. Deep within my dreams that thought gave me a scare and your presence is what startled me awake.

PERFIDY: Am I always to blame for the things that bring you pain? I thought I was the source of your pleasure.

RAIN: You are.

PERFIDY: I returned simply to explain that my need for you journeys beyond measure.

RAIN: *(Rising, she crosses to the window. She is wearing simple bedclothes.)* I doubted your return. You never even called.

PERFIDY: I had business that needed attending. But I am here now. With you. And I'm appalled that you insist on pretending you're not happy to see me. I can't believe that's true. Perhaps you should come back to bed. Then we can discuss all that you've been through and the silly thoughts that rattle in your head.

RAIN: *(Becoming angered)* You think I spent my days languished at your loss. While you're away I am void of any matter. You think I spent time mourning that our paths would never cross. That without you my life would simply shatter. I find your arrogance unbecoming at best.

PERFIDY: *(Rising from the bed)* You misread me. My words bear no insult. What I, in fact, was trying to suggest was that you missed me and as a result you feared, as you said, that I would not return. But I am here as if I'd never gone. So you see, there is neither cause for your concern nor the conclusions that you've drawn. *(He crosses to her. Rain crosses away, down center.)*

RAIN: Minutes passed for hours. Days passed for weeks. Funny how capricious time can be. Despite its composition the calendar speaks no truth, harbors no consistency. *(She turns to face him.)* Only a moment has elapsed in your world, and in that moment nothing has changed. In mine, more than an eternity unfurled and my whole life has since been re-arranged. So if I have written an inaccurate conclusion the culpability rests on time. I refuse to accept the blame for my confusion. I refuse to confess to any crime.

PERFIDY: *(Taking her hands in his)* With such labor in your thoughts you're bound to be perplexed. There's only fiction in what you create. The finale that you write has no basis in the text of reality. So I will set you straight. *(He places her arms around his waste, then cups her face in his hands.)* Your face beneath my palm is warm. You

24

crumble at my touch. *(He draws his hands down her neck, shoulders, arms, then rests them on her hips.)* What I breathe out you eagerly inhale. You want me. *(His hands slide behind her, caressing her buttocks as he moves his mouth closer to hers.)*

RAIN: No.

PERFIDY: *(Closer still)* You want me.

RAIN: *(Breaking the embrace)* I don't need you as my crutch. Your hands are cold and your breath is stale.

PERFIDY: *(Angered, but maintaining some restraint)* My presence has unbalanced you so you are reprieved of your indiscretions, though I am disheartened. When I arrived, I must admit, I truly believed you would welcome me in your heart again. What must I say to convince you that my need is great? Do you wish...love...to whisper in my kiss?

RAIN: I wish the truth.

PERFIDY: The truth won't come if you manipulate, and love means nothing if this coercion brings it about.

RAIN: It was you who mentioned love. It was you who came to me in my sleep. It was you who went away.

PERFIDY: *(Showing more of his anger)* Do you wish to shove me further away or keep me by your side? It's your choice. You decide. But I warn you, be sure of what you choose. Should you elect to push me aside then know full well that you will lose all the components that make you complete. And this time I won't come along to pick up the pieces as they lie at your feet and put them neatly back where they belong.

RAIN: Is that why you are here? To replace and secure all the parts that in your absence have come loose? Then I will whimper at your whim and you can be sure I will eagerly submit to your abuse?

PERFIDY: *(Grabbing Rain by the shoulders in anger. He shakes her.)* You insolent bitch! You pathetic little fool! Without me you are no more than a ghost! You have no mind of your own. You force me to rule over your body which is nothing but a host to what I create. Do you understand?!

RAIN: *(Afraid)* Your clutch is tight. Please, you're hurting me.

PERFIDY: *(His grip remains. His anger grows.)* You succeed in ruining all that I have planned. This is not how it was supposed to be!

RAIN: Forgive me for bringing ruin to your artifice. How could I know such a plan was in place? Great thought was required to build this edifice of deception. Was your goal to disgrace me into crumbling to my knees, and while there to bring pleasure to your manhood?

PERFIDY: *(He slaps her face. Her reaction is cool. He turns ice cold.)* What you have ruined you cannot repair and your effort to shock me is no good. There was a time when my standing before you willingly brought you to your knees. I wish you happiness. But there is nothing I can do.

RAIN: It isn't me you wish to please.

PERFIDY: *(Releasing her from his grip)* Impertinence runs quickly from your brain to your lips. You know nothing of the things you say. I grow tired of your insults. Am bored with your quips. I'm not concerned with the games that you play. Exhaustion comes not with the love that we

26

make, but with the battles that are fought before the fact. This time I will have what I have come to take before you destroy it with this act. *(He grabs her and kisses her. She breaks the embrace. He grabs her tighter and kisses her harder. She tries to break free but he lifts her from the ground, crosses to the bed and drops her down.)* Don't waste your energy putting up a fight. You know it's always the same in the end.

RAIN: *(Struggling)* No! I don't.

PERFIDY: I thought that you might struggle and try to defend what you think of as virtue, which doesn't exist, for I have stripped you of that long ago. Don't fight me, Rain. There's no need to resist.

RAIN: Perfidy...please...let me go!

PERFIDY: Look me in the eye and tell me you don't care. Under the touch of my hand can you deny that you are driven with lust.

RAIN: *(Crying)* You're not being fair.

PERFIDY: Don't bother. It won't help to cry. I've seen those tears before. You use them as a tool to influence how I feel. But you forget that I am not a fool and what you think you want isn't real. *(She is audibly struggling now.)* Damn you! Be quiet! Your words are distracting. Your dramatic attempts to break free make me laugh. You really are over-acting.

RAIN: I'm begging you...please...let me be! *(She starts to kick, breaks free and leaps from the bed. He grabs her quickly and throws her back down. She is crying)*

PERFIDY: Shut up! You little girl. You rotten little beast!

RAIN: I don't want this. Please let me go.

27

PERFIDY: You will take what I give you. *(She is struggling hard.)* On you I will feast! *(He pulls on her hair. She screams. He slaps her face hard.)*

RAIN: No! Oh God, no! *(She bites him. He is shocked by the sudden pain and releases her.)*

PERFIDY: You bit me! *(He rises from the bed)* Fine! I don't want to demand your affections. It's clear your desire for me has died. I haven't the strength to bear your rejections. You have shattered my will. Though I've tried to reach beyond your veneer, encompass your soul, you choose to live behind this facade. So I will leave for this match has taken its toll on my heart *(He is yelling)* on which you carelessly trod! *(He crosses to the door.)*

RAIN: Wait! *(She opens her mouth as if to speak but no words come out.)*

PERFIDY: *(He stops)* What do you want? Another twist in your game. Or are you simply grasping at straws?

RAIN: *(Hesitates slightly)* I want to hear in your voice as you call out my name, without judgment or hate, without pause that you love me.

PERFIDY: *(Crossing back to the bed, having won)* Fickle girl living in a fairy tale. But I'll give you what you want as you request.
RAIN: You must mean it from your heart or else you will fail.

PERFIDY: I had no idea this was a test. Once your ears are filled with the words you wish to hear will you then end this tiresome game of chase? Or will new rules be created to which I must adhere?

RAIN: Your sarcasm can not erase the fact that you are unable to admit your love for me.

28

PERFIDY: I am able to do a great deal. What I choose to do is the issue, don't you see. I won't let you walk in and steal control of my heart. It's mine and mine alone.

RAIN: But you have mine. So that means you have two. If I had yours I would care for it as if it were my own. But, I have none. What would you have me do?

PERFIDY: *(Crossing back to the door)* Foolish, don't you think, to give away one thing just to hunger for another in its place. You must deal with that yourself. Do not attempt to bring me this problem which I choose not to face. *(He opens the door as if to leave.)* Goodbye, Rain. I don't expect I'll see you again. No tangible mass is left to touch. Of what we once had, of what might have been, a penumbra remains...and that's not much.

RAIN: I love you...Perfidy...Isn't that enough?

PERFIDY: *(Scoffing)* It means nothing if I own your heart. Once I might have stayed. But today I call your bluff. And take my advice, you'd be smart to remember the mistakes that you've made that provoked the end to this romance. When you're alone, ask the question, was the price that you paid worth it? If only you could have known in advance of all the things that would bring about the fall of everything I've made, of all I've have built. What would you do, if you had any brains at all, to avoid being left with only guilt? *(He opens the door as if to leave.)*

RAIN: Anything you ask.

PERFIDY: What?

RAIN: I'll do anything you ask. Just promise me you'll stay a moment more.

PERFIDY: No more questions? No more games? For you a noble task.

RAIN: Just as long as you don't walk out that door.

PERFIDY: Very well. *(He closes the door and crosses back to the bed. He sits beside Rain and touches her hair.)* Promise the next time I come by you'll abandon these ridiculous impressions. Don't waste my time with aimless words. Promise me you'll try to make these more satisfying sessions. *(He kisses her.)* Do you love me?

RAIN: Yes. *(He kisses her.)*

PERFIDY: Think of me incessantly?

RAIN: Yes.

PERFIDY: In every thought? In all you do?

RAIN: Yes...always. I think about you constantly.

PERFIDY: You love me.

RAIN: Yes. I love you. Do you love me?

PERFIDY: You promised. No questions. No games. Really, Rain...I've taken on the part of the trainer and you are the lion that he tames. I never liked that role from the start.

RAIN: I'm sorry.

PERFIDY: Good. Now close your eyes and relax.

RAIN: I want to see you.

PERFIDY: You'll see me from inside. I'll know you love me in how your body reacts. You'll convince me you have nothing to hide. *(He climbs on top of her. The lights fade to black. In the darkness a door is heard opening and closing. The lights come up to dim. Rain is standing by the window in the same simple bedclothes she wore earlier. She crosses back to the bed and lies down. A spotlight shines on the window. Perfidy is standing outside looking in. Rain moves restlessly in bed. Perfidy smiles.)*

BLACKOUT

THE END

Dark as Water in Winter

poems

THE KITCHEN TABLE

The kitchen table was a hand-me-down,
a gift of sorts, from my mother's mother,
acquired when the family moved uptown
into a home separate from the other

relatives. She hated it, the table,
with napkin drawer hung underneath, and just
too small for us children to be able
to sit around at holidays. *Why must*

I always have to settle? she would say
while cleaning up the hardened beef and egg,
decaying Brussels sprouts I hid away
inside the napkin drawer. Sometimes she'd beg

my Dad to buy a "dining" table, one
with leaves that would extend to fit us all,
mahogany, shiny, as if the sun
were reflecting off the finish, and tall-

backed chairs and hutch to match and not a nick
or scratch or grease-stain from spilled oatmeal left
neglected by the baby-sitter. *Sick
and tired of the mess* she'd sigh bereft

of joy, even though we'd kiss her face, flushed
from holding back the tears. We were seven
in a tiny house, and the burden crushed
my mother. *I'm sure to die young, heaven*

knows. In dreams I'd stand before her casket.
Laid to rest in rubber gloves and splattered
crusty egg. I held for her a basket
of cold cooked Brussels sprouts which I scattered

on the silk beside her body. I dreamed
she was happy being dead and I cried
myself awake. Her eyes were black. They seemed
to hold onto every moment in wide,

eternal disappointment, although there
were moments when they'd sparkle, mostly when
the moments were her own. Those times were rare.
She would sit at the table then, a pen

to paper, writing down her pain in short
stories that she called fiction, but I knew
the emotion was true. Often she'd court
a happy ending but she always threw

it away, leaving the story broken.
She'd start new ones, which she'd never fulfill.
Some regarded her words as a token
or extravagance. But I saw them spill

out onto the page, intense, fierce, hard.
What she released in writing she never
gave to us. The table took the brunt. Marred
with the faint imprint of a name, clever

phrase or angry thought when her pen was gripped
too tight. He never saw her write, my Dad.
When his car pulled in the driveway, she slipped
her feelings in the napkin drawer. Her pen and pad

neatly out of view in the same place where
I hid my Brussels sprouts. And though compelled,
we never spoke of secrets we would share
or the kitchen table where they were held.

SOMETHING FOR FLORENCE
a pantoum

A milky film over old, teary eyes.
Through the haze she reviews an abstract world.
Clarity held in her lap counting beads,
Florence soundlessly mouths her private prayers.

Through the haze she reviews an abstract world.
A stranger comes, lays kisses on her cheeks.
Florence soundlessly mouths her private prayers
and wonders why her husband doesn't call.

A stranger comes, lays kisses on her cheeks.
Where's Armand? Reply. *He's dead now.* She cries
and wonders why her husband doesn't call.
A nurse checks her pulse and her morphine patch.

Where's Armand? Reply. *He's dead now.* She cries.
Tries to stretch her legs but they're hard to move.
A nurse checks her pulse and her morphine patch.
I had the nicest gams in town you know.

Tries to stretch her legs but they're hard to move.
The nurse nods, says she's told her that before.
I had the nicest gams in town you know.
From her chair by the window, *I could dance.*

The nurse nods, says she's told her that before.
At eighty-nine it's hard to see today
from her chair by the window. *I could dance.*
She jitterbugs with Armand in her mind.

At eighty-nine it's hard to see today.
Can't dress or wash herself or write to friends.
She jitterbugs with Armand in her mind,
numbed by the anesthesia of the past.

Can't dress or wash herself or write to friends.
Her hands, they're good for just one thing these days.
Numbed by the anesthesia of the past,
there's nothing left for Florence here except

her hands. They're good for just one thing these days.
Clarity held in her lap, counting beads.
There's nothing left for Florence here except
a milky film over old, teary eyes.

MÉMÈRE

She was plump, that's all I knew, and gray.
Grew rhubarb in the backyard and made
delicious afternoons. In her day

Mom says her bright red hair and legs turned
heads. Her wiles illumined in her smile,
beguiling freckled face that returned

with glory on her youngest child. She,
like me, liked uncluttered things. Simple
seamstress made us all look good. I see

her in the mirror. Just a glimmer
sometimes, when I'm most content. Pretty
Mémère reflected in the shimmer

of sheers in open windows. Lifted
in the scent of fresh baked rhubarb pie.
Present in the hugs of her gifted

daughters. Winter evenings, now and then,
before the hearth, warmed by a well-stoked
fire, wrapped in the afghan, crocheted when

we were babies, I feel her sitting
across the room, reading short stories
from the Reader's Digest or knitting.

And in portraits on my parents' wall
a brand new bride stands beside a brand
new groom. He was mustached, lanky, tall.

She was lovely, slender, sweet. Their lives
created generations, children,
grand, great and great-great. And each arrives,

an extension of her. Together,
the family enjoyed Cape Cod clam bakes
and chronic sunshine and hot weather

at Florida beaches. In the dry breeze
she wore short sleeves and short pants. Just off
the shore on the grass, under the trees

we'd lay our blanket, plant chairs and play.
In the shade she'd shine and Mom would say her bright
red hair and legs turned heads in her day.

She was plump, that's all I knew, and gray.
Grew rhubarb in the backyard and made
delicious afternoons. Sweet Mémère.

ENTERING MASSACHUSETTS
a villanelle

Rest stop, fast food, toilet, gas station,
toll booth, police car, towering street light,
half-burned out woodland lines the highway

vehicles laden for vacation
strapped on bikes on roofs, balance upright,
rest stop, fast food, toilet, gas station.

Sun disappears on a Worcester day
as if to say it's not worth the fight.
Half burned-out woodland lines the highway.

Trucks, campers, Jeeps seek recreation
while always keeping the state in sight.
Rest stop, fast food, toilet, gas station

pretending to thank me for my stay
but traps me in Brockton overnight.
Half burned-out woodland lines the highway

marking my route in cold formation.
How long to pass through? Someday I might.
Rest stop, fast food, toilet, gas station,
half burned-out woodland lines the highway.

41

SELF-PORTRAIT
a rhyme royale

If I create a wondrous piece, surround
it by a pure white mat and gold leaf frame,
and hang it low upon a wall, astound
the most discerning eye and set aflame
the coldest heart, arrest the feral, tame
the wild, then...I'd direct the world to see
a thing that's beautiful instead of me.

If I could set the perfect word beside
the perfect word, and string a thought into
a line, and swing the morning sun inside
a rhyme, caress the wind with softest hue
that paint the clouds alliterating blue
and pink, then...lovely lilting verses might
convince the reader I am what I write.

To picture pulchritude is mere desire.
Reality presents an ugly fact.
To blind the world I must become a liar,
dependent on how others will react.
Delusions found in art, though somewhat cracked,
have always held a beauty in their flaws.
So I must work to carry out this cause

to draw away attention from my face,
and put it on a wall or in a book.
A wondrous piece created in the place
of that which I despise. And I, the rook,
shall step outside myself, so those who look
will be distracted long enough to see
a thing that's beautiful instead of me.

QUIETING EILEEN

Hush, hush Eileen. You talk too much.
You speak your mind more than you should.
Don't cry how you're misunderstood.
Not everyone has interest.

Please, please Eileen. A bit of peace.
Give us a moment if you will.
Your voice this night is awfully shrill.
Some silence is a welcomed rest.

Come, come Eileen. Don't be so glum.
It's not the first time you've been told
to shut your mouth. I hate to scold
but I've no desire to invest

in your squabbles or your babble,
your banter, blather, chattering.
It isn't very flattering
to spew your verbal vomit. Lest

you wish to be known a fool, cruel,
in fact. Indeed that is your choice.
But as long as we hear your voice
I shall do more than to request

you learn to become taciturn.
You see, my dear, you interfere
with our opinions, and we fear,
you may display to know what's best.

There, there Eileen. It isn't fair
that you should be intelligent,
perceived as being eloquent
It's easier, you may have guessed,

for us to shine in ignorance,
opinionated impudence
and overstated arrogance
without your having to protest

each word you've heard. We've worked quite hard
to convince the illiterate
they are, to us, inadequate.
You understand how we detest

your reasoning. Now, now Eileen,
we must insist you let us reach
the smallest minds with aimless speech.
They're much more readily impressed.

A WALK AWAY

A slow descent to graveled walk,
barefooted. Jagged path reflect
the passage into dusk. Neglect
the logical direction. Talk
to me about me without you.

It's fine when we are face-to-face,
skin-to-skin and heart-to-bone,
but afterward when I'm alone,
I long to feel our last embrace.
A me that's now me without you.

Ephemeral, not meant to be.
A momentary unity.
A fleeting, careless parity
that breaks apart the second we
divide into me without you.

Each stone embeds itself in stride.
Each stride creates a deeper cut.
My wandering can't give me what
will fill the hollow deep inside
that comes from the me without you.

I think I'm walking with the sun.
I fool myself and trudge ahead
but find you far behind instead.
And I, as night that's just begun,
am one in the me without you.

PHOTOGRAPH
a villanelle

I took a photograph of him in silhouette,
the center of his back against a concrete wall.
He sat below the awning to avoid the rain.

Vague profile in tattered layers refused to let
the world inside his world that grew forever small.
I took a photograph of him in silhouette

wanting the details of his features to remain
in shadow, like his presence, like rats, like nightfall.
He sat below the awning to avoid the rain.

The steam from sewer grates and subway holes offset
edifices lined in rows, miles wide and miles tall.
I took a photograph of him in silhouette

behind the blurry pedestrians, who made sane
the city street, walked with backbeat car horn, cab call.
He sat below the awning to avoid the rain.

His home is here. He's found his place and pays his debt
by staying. Every day he's passed, unseen by all.
I took a photograph of him in silhouette.
He sits below the awning to avoid the rain.

TRUTH AND THE
ICE CREAM TRUCK

a triolet

So when the chime rang I scrambled to collect some change,
pennies, dimes lost on the street, found in a sofa seat.
Twenty-five cents was more than Mom or Dad could arrange.
So when the chime ran I scrambled to collect some change,
knowing not to ask for fear I would estrange
myself even more, and anyway, not get the sweet.
So when the chime rang I scrambled to collect some change,
pennies, dimes lost on the street, found in a sofa seat.

At the curb a neighborhood converged with a dollar
in each fist. Capricious banter filled the summer air.
Get the chocolate chip ice cream sandwich, one would holler.
At the curb a neighborhood converged with a dollar
to spend on anything. *Almond crunch bar*, a smaller
voice would shout. I stood, coins in hand, quietly aware
at the curb. A neighborhood converged with a dollar
in each fist. Capricious banter filled the summer air.

The truck overflowed with dreams of frozen cakes and cream.
Lemon ice, I'd say. Pay my pittance. Always the same
ritual. Two-bits clattered on the counter and gleam. I'd beam.
The truck overflowed with dreams of frozen cakes and cream,
and though the milk, soft, truffle treats were tempting, I would
deem
that this one lasted longest. I knew from where I came.
The truck overflowed with dreams of frozen cakes and cream.
Lemon ice, I'd say. Pay my pittance. Always the same.

A LADY

an English sonnet

At first we feel her, then the wave begins.
Our focus on her entrance through the door.
The turn of heads congruent with the pins
and needles on our necks. She glides before
our wanting-hating eyes and casts a kind
but knowing glance with lips upturned. Yet all
we do is stare as she walks by. Refined
in step, her fingers brush the air and call
attention to her hips. And as her black
hair bountifully frames her fair-skinned face
and flounces playfully across her back,
we raise our hands self-conscious in our place
to touch our faces and our hair. Prefer
to be all that we love and hate in her.

WOMAN IN THE DARK
a triolet

She's pretty in the dark,
as pretty as she wants to be.
Lonely little lark.
She's pretty in the dark,
glistening in the spark
of fancy-filled obscurity.
She's pretty in the dark.
As pretty as she wants to be.

STORM CLOUDS

Clouds are resting on the mountains
weary from the midday rainfall,
swollen from the thunder's painful
beating on the atmosphere.
Gullies forming into fountains
as torrential tantrums deplete
their blackened bellies and make sweet
the valley air.

WITHOUT WATER

When endless golden fields of wheat
had proudly waved their hearty hailing,
the sky succumbed to clouds replete
with rain and thunder rolls regaling.
We bowed our heads to God and earth
while praises raised in crackling mirth,
could not anticipated the heat
nor drown impending droughts unveiling.

Disinterested overcast
dispersed as final droplets faded.
And stalks and roots had drunk the last
of what so amply once cascaded.
The day held fast then held its breath
and noon became the hour of death,
for unforgiving sun had passed
its hand across the land unshaded.

Now crops are dropping to their knees,
a fever climbing ever steeper.
And crumbled under arid breeze
is dust forsaken by its keeper.
No angels swoop to lift the face
or saturate the soil with grace.
We rail the rising grim degrees
and mourn the passing of the reaper.

WILTING
Haiku

forlorn zinnias
with heads dropped over, mourning
in the morning sun

IRIS

an English sonnet

Erect upon her stem she blossoms tall,
as petals, orange, softly layered, fold
around each other, stroke the stalk and fall
aside. Reveal a heart of deepest gold.
The evening rain has moistened her inside
and droplets linger on her velvet pleats.
They puddle briefly, then begin to glide
along her body and the wind completes
her. Sweet aroma in the afterglow
enraptures. She is naked, open, full.
This is the most she'll be, the most she'll grow
before she fades, succumbs to nature's pull.
But in this moment sensual perfume
awakes the soul that makes love with the bloom.

NINE-TENTHS OF THE LAW
a tanka

Do I own the rose
because I captured its scent,
and covet its blush,
or does the garden possess
the deed and I merely rent?

AUTUMN NIGHTS AND
LITTLE THINGS

Underneath the wooden stair,
below the pumpkin, bottom rotting,
kitten sleeps most unaware
of the fury in the air.
Silently she's dreaming there
of romps and kills, of chase and plotting.

During late-day autumn sun
the leaves arise in blissful breezes.
Passers-by ride bikes and run
side-by-side. Their tossing fun
caught by nearly everyone,
with laughter passed like season's sneezes.

Looming night, the light retreats.
A mother anxiously is calling
to her children in the streets.
Beckoning them home, she meets
each one at the door. Completes
her task just as the black is falling.

Settled on a cul-de-sac,
the mother's jarring beets, preserving
fruit. Beyond the street out back,
neighbor's built a wooden shack,
where a boy's seen through the crack
interring items. Quite unnerving.

Still, this small suburban place
invites the overworked and weary
to recline in peaceful grace,
some before the fireplace,
others in a safe embrace,
to ward off darkness. Damp and dreary.

Doors are locked. The prayers are said.
The little ones secured from danger.
Mother checks beneath the bed
for the monsters that were bred
out of stories that were read,
and of a being even stranger.

Something's come these past few weeks.
It preys at night on tiny creatures.
None surmise and no one speaks
of the howls and the shrieks,
of the way the back porch creaks,
leaving prints of child-like features.

Hallowed, harvest moon awakes
a menace that evokes revulsion.
Wanders through the yards and breaks
through the bolted gates. He takes
breaths as cold as snow and makes
his way to sate his odd compulsion.

Dawn delivers cloudy skies
and tokens from this shadow-dweller.
Near the morning paper lies
tiny entrails, bones and eyes,
on a pile of stones as flies
invade the mother's home and cellar.

Now beneath the wooden stair
a kitten twitches in her sleeping.
Crack of twigs sound through the air,
crunching ever closer where
kitten dreams most unaware,
while the neighbor's boy comes creeping.

THE FORGIVING SEASON
an English sonnet

When sun is hanging purple in the sky
and snow reflects the passage of the day,
when naked arms of apple trees stretch high
above the silver dusk, and fingers sway
to song of Solstice, Christmas choirs and bells
from distant churches, memories begin
a shift to times that don't exist. When swells
of seasons greetings ring through fragile, thin
and penetrating air, a dreaming takes
control of me, and thoughts of happy times
become reality. Erase mistakes,
replenish virtue, pardon crimes with rhymes
that quickly trip from lips and whisper cheer.
This is a most forgiving time of year.

FOOTPRINTS IN THE SNOW

an English sonnet

I walk along the bank of snowy stream
and try to find a shallow place to cross,
but drifts collect upon each branch and seem
to purposefully trap me with my loss.
I haven't the desire to fight the flow,
nor have I the intent to go alone,
so why I wander here I do not know.
Perhaps it is the coldness of the stone
or crackle of the icy brush beneath
my shoes, the bitter wind that grips my throat,
colliding cries with chattering of teeth.
A winter song that travels this remote
embankment blankets, comforts my caprice.
I walk with memories of you in peace.

THE SCREAMING

I thought the scream before I let it go.
Imagined already large and frightened
eyes explode with horror at the sudden force
of scream. Charted the churning, spiraled course
that Providence could not change. Enlightened

simply by fascination of the scream.
Envisioned you, a child's breath more than five,
gasping for air, reeling back. Size-kid feet
giving out to buckled knees. Saw it beat
against your flesh, take form. And I, alive

twice your time, should not have been pleased
to watch tender palms, thin arms hit the floor
before the rest of you. I felt the scream
twist in my stomach, lived it like a dream
as it climbed the back-side of my throat, more

choking than rope. I knew what it would do.
You whimpered, young boy whimpers for help. Eyes
wide, you cowered against where wall meets wall,
allowed whitewashed backdrop to cup your small
frame, while I stood dumb, slapped with cries

that fell from lips that should only ever
know the sweet taste of fresh blown sugar and
candied apples and Italian ice. At
that moment you looked at me from where you sat
with a knowing I knew well of me. Hand

to mouth, I stood, a clown, ghoulish
in my dramatic stance, foolish to think
I could stop the scream. You were innocent
in the juncture right before the scream. Meant
to be naïve. You shattered in the blink

between where light turns black, quiet stillness
turns to chaos with sudden explosive
destructive TNT, once bound now freed.
Ten thousand pounds of power emptied
over your lightly tanned skin. Corrosive

outcry that ate away your innocence.
I thought the scream and then I let it go.
Dark shadows swelled below your already
large and frightened eyes. An ever steady
chin quivered, while a sallow dulled the glow

that once glazed your sun-kissed cheeks. A child's breath
more than five. You held the scream that raped youth
from your years, and carried it with you. I
became the echo of the scream. The cry
you could not hide. The screaming of the truth.

SHE CAN'T COME OUT TO PLAY TODAY

a villanelle

Wasted day for the little girl, musing
through time, shut away in her upstairs room,
while two squirrels dance about the yard below.

Pleasant how the creatures play amusing
games of chase. She studies them from her tomb.
Wasted day for the little girl musing

of escape out the double-paned window.
Restricted to her chair, shackled by gloom,
while two squirrels dance about the yard below.

Hopeful sunshine just beyond her choosing
teases with spring breezes and sweet perfume.
Wasted day for the little girl musing

she can fly. Her broken mind a shadow
once defined as sharp. Rocking in her womb
while two squirrels dance about the yard below.

No rope, no bars, no padlock. Refusing
to descend, she looks forward to her doom.
Wasted day for the little girl, musing,
while two squirrels dance about the yard below.

AMANDA KEEPS A SECRET

an envelope sonnet

Amanda has a secret and she's scared.
She hides it tucked away inside her spleen,
kept undetected from the world, between
her stomach and her diaphragm. Ensnared
in lies, the crime divides, expanding in
the blood. It spawns a panic and a dread
that magnifies regret inside her head
and threatens to expose this mortal sin,
this parasite that feeds on guilt. It grows
within her abdomen. Enraged, too strong
to be concealed, it rips her skin. She cries
alone and grips the sleeping pills. She knows
it can not be undone or hidden long,
and so the secret with Amanda dies.

THE STEALING OF
A WINTER HEART
an English sonnet

He carries cold inside his coat beside
a heart, once fanciful, at present grave.
His hand, the left, is hidden, slipped inside
unbuttoned folds, as if to hold and save
and stroke a scared abandoned kitten, though
it really cups an ebbing beat. I see
the fabric rise and fall. He doesn't know
it's obvious the motion comes from me.
A stolen heart replaces his. He took
it while I slept. Disposed his own across
my chest where it expired. So now I look
at vain attempts to vitalize my loss.
He grips my heart in feeble fist to try
and pump a life I'm sure is doomed to die.

BETTER LEFT UNSAID
couplets

I'm frightened of the things I think,
of crippling thoughts that rise and sink
inside already aching head
from too much drink and what was said.

The words were few and briefly soared.
The wine was plenty, freely poured.
Consumed in pallid parlor light,
consuming spirits through the night,

I felt the murmur soft and low
tap dancing on my tongue, and so
I let it slip past tooth and lip
in whispers no more than a quip.

It seemed a simple thing to say
and thought the words would go away
in moments after they escaped.
But here they are again, reshaped,

to fit a meaning all their own.
And here I am, unarmed, alone,
teetering on the edge of death,
repeating it in waning breath.

I pray that I shall die tonight.
I pray to die with all my might.
If only it weren't said aloud.
If only I were not so proud,

the angels, then, may not have heard,
construed the meaning word for word.
I pray that I shall die tonight.
I pray to die with all my might.

My heartbeat slows in weighted chest
with chilling sweat between each breast
and freezing images of Hell
form under jaded eyes. The knell

tolls as the howling wolf, distant
hooting owl and persistent
crickets' dirge, while hallowed
omens lurk in dusty shadowed

corners. Certain in the hours
when drunken fever overpowers
sensibility, a fateful
phrase was uttered in a hateful

daze. Sins replaying on the wall
collect with cobwebs. I recall
in great detail each deed, each crime.
Condemned for what I've done and I'm

afraid. Deadly invocation
answered without hesitation.
I pray that I shall die tonight.
I pray to die with all my might.

Summoned suicidal specter
once too often. As the nectar
plays its fatal games on a brain
now saturated and insane,

dreams ignite a nightmare. Not sure
of what is real or not. What's more
I can't recant, I can't negate
my fervent plea, so I await

my destiny. While demons creep
the chanting drifts into sleep.
I pray that I shall die tonight.
I pray to die with all my might.

DIPSOMANIA
an English sonnet

When hurt finds refuge in a silent heart
and past replays its darkest moments in
a mind that's bound by lack of spark, in part
from heritage, in part because of sin,
these are the times in which I'm forced to live.
So when I have but me to draw upon
to numb, insensate, I can only give
a fleeting vision of a blinding dawn,
and hope the day eradicates the night.
And when the night becomes too much to bear
I drown the dreaded moon, imbibe the light
from dregs that line a bottle of despair.
I hate myself come morning, sick and real,
when forced, again, to face myself and feel.

EBONY DREAM

I wish I were black, as dark as water
in winter, as deep as a Georgia night
when the moon is new, as when thoughts of you,
darkened by mounds of dirt don't hurt, and light
is other than white. I wish I were black

with a caramel voice that sings each word
that hums when heard and releases the might
of a hundred years. If only your ears
could hear what I wish I could sing, delight
in the song carried on strong currents back

and forth from my heart to yours. I'd awake
old spirits, create new souls that take flight
in dance, inspire, set fire to the whole world.
I wish I were black, as rich and as right
as an African panther, whose attack,

instinctive, patient maneuvers, flawless
stealth, caresses the ground with prey in sight,
comes from a need to survive not succeed.
Artisan-crafted eyes, smile would shine bright
in the absence of my face. But I lack

the beauty which lives in black. Am without
its virtuous veracity despite
these lines that glare on fair skin, show each sin.
I'd hold heritage in my arms, ignite
words into poetry if I were black.

I wish I were you. I wish I were. Wish.
I wish I could be not me. Just a slight
reflection of a dark complexion. In
mirrors I wish to see someone not quite
the one I've come to know as me. To crack

the glass and feel between the breaks. Welcome
the face of black. I would live in the bright
sun, not afraid to be near anyone,
too close to you. A part of you. You might
have loved me. You might have. If I were black.

PIECEMEAL

I don't remember you.
A face that I once knew,
pale blue eyes, sometimes green,
when days were young between
the years when we were too.

I can't create your face
or recognize the place
where we once laughed and played
and touched and dreamed and made
memories to embrace.

White smile that held the sky,
a wit that made me cry.
Golden hair that would shine
when touched with sun, so fine
it floated on a sigh.

The pieces break apart
when taken from my heart
to arrange on the floor
and see you stand before
me whole. The cracks that chart

your death are clear, and now
I fear, I can't somehow
remember you, except
in pieces that I've kept
in drawers. Although I vow

today to not forget
and live without regret,
I can't live up to what
you were. Nothing left but
for the fragments. I set

aside your hand. Slender
fingers hold in tender
embrace the ring he slipped
when no one looked. Thin-lipped
grin, steady chin. Gender

same. You came to be truth
in a false world. Your youth
was the crime you died for.
Residuum. Just your
effigy. Hand and tooth.

Leg and brow. Replicate
your body. Indicate
a whisper. Recover
words quipped to your lover.
Record. Then extricate

the memory. And when
sleep, out of reach again
sits on the carpet near
the bed. Tapping. I hear
sleep tap the brass post. Ten.

Midnight. Two a.m. Sleep
taps the brass post. I weep
to the rhythm. Awake
heavy. You laugh and break
the cadence, and you creep

into a waking dream.
For a moment you seem
real. In that moment right
below where sleep and night
become submerged in cream-

colored fantasy. Just
then I taste your voice. Trust
your wink. Hold the shadow,
the blink, the dim, hollow
happy past. And I must

but can't remember you.
As space grows wider, due
to time, you'll fade, splinter
I won't see your winter
skin, stylish shoes. The few

items I hold now will
disappear, and the still
lightless landscape that used
to be your life, though bruised
and hopeful, often ill,

will be all I possess
of you. So, I confess,
I long to keep the bits,
the glimpses, glimmers. It's
better than nothingness.

I'll treasure your ember,
each changing December
your echo, your vestige,
diminishing image,
but I can't remember.

ALONE WITH HER INIQUITY

Tangled in a midnight gloom,
mantled in a musty room,
lives betrayer and betrayed.
Festering she picks apart,
piece by piece, an errant heart
while the madness makes its start
in the lair where liars laid.

Here amidst the fragments find
what was once a lucid mind,
what was once a woman whole.
Silken skin and sable hair,
remnants of a lady fair.
Fell to lust, awoke despair.
Fooled with love and lost her soul.

DEPRESSION AT MY DOOR

an English sonnet

My winter friend came calling in the night
equipped with candied fruit and too much wine.
Surpassing spring. Obliterating light.
Prepared a sorrow stew so we could dine
on melancholy. Seasoned it with fear
that I would not survive without him, so
I bade him stay. He wiped away my tear.
and poured a glass, then drew the shade to low
the morning sun. We toasted death. I held
his hand and cried and could not see beyond
the mellowed drink. Familiar comfort swelled
with every sip. I slipped into a fond
depressive state and fought the need for rest.
Dependent on my most invited guest.

AWAKENING
a pantoum

The morning lays a little lighter on the bed,
the angry sun a little brighter on my chest,
as if it can't find cause to be hateful to me.
So I rise and brush my teeth and begin the day.

The angry sun, a little brighter on my chest,
lingers through my shower and sours my breakfast tea.
I rise, brush my teeth, once again begin the day.
Press your pillow to my face, inhale to erase

what lingered through my shower, soured my breakfast tea.
Your sweet aroma turns to nectar on my lips
your pillow to my face, I inhale to erase
haunting images of the lives I've lived before.

Your sweet aroma turns to nectar on my lips
and with it comes the vestige of the familiar
haunting images of the lives I've lived before.
I wear your favorite tee-shirt underneath my vest

and with it comes the vestige of the familiar
comfort felt when our dreams are lying side-by-side.
I wear your favorite tee-shirt underneath my vest
so my heartbeat will touch what touches you. And I

feel the comfort of our dreams lying side-by-side
and the day can't find cause to be hateful to me
when you touch my heartbeat, when it touches you. And
the morning lays a little lighter on the bed.

THE PASSING
couplets

It was the twenty-sixth of June.
The clouds that shrouded mournful moon,
by sudden gust of summer wind,
dispersed with everything I'd sinned.
In moments right before the dawn,
when all I was was all but gone,
the universe had opened wide.
For on this day in June I died.

SEEING THROUGH THE MOST BEAUTIFUL EYES
a kyrielle

Why do you look so sad my love?
he asks with compassionate eyes,
clover green, clear as rain. Above
the trees I see the clouds. He sighs
and he kisses my face and says,

See that woman across the way,
in her mohair coat and bright pink
lipstick. She looks pretty today
and that makes her happy, I think.
Wipes a tear from my face and says,

See that man coming from the store.
I bet he bought grapes, and I bet
they're sweet. We'll buy grapes, and eat more
than we should, and sleep when we get
full. He touches my face and says,

See what I see. Find joy in things
so small they'd likely be ignored,
like little cats attacking strings,
like eating oysters, being bored,
and dreams. He holds my face and says,

See, my love, the sun is breaking
through the ashen sky just for you.
She's shining to mend your aching
heart. As the gray gives way to blue
he settles on my face and says,

So follow my gaze and you'll see
what makes me smile. And I realize
he hasn't stopped looking at me.
Then says through sparkling clover eyes,
I love you. And kisses my face.

DANCING IN A SIMPLE PARADISE
a terza rima

Her hand in his, she spun around the chair.
Her thin legs, brown beneath an airborne skirt,
became as weightless as her long black hair.

They danced just inches from the pool. He'd flirt
with her, and she'd flirt back, with smiles that glowed
like newborn moonlight in between a spurt

of stars. Enchanting, winsome play. She'd goad
him into giggling. A gentle prod
that brought a blush. We watched him as he showed

his guilelessness. A tender, simple nod
that held Maria long enough to let
her go. So there I sat, the tourist, flawed

beneath my gift-shop shades and soaking wet
bikini, enamored by their honesty.
She made the drinks, refilled the chips, then set

a salsa bowl between the majesty
of daiquiris and straws and fruit. He brushed
her arm to reach the tray. Their modesty

secure inside their youth. He turned and rushed
to serve familiar people he had served
the day before while splashing water hushed

the breeze. *She's beautiful,* you had observed.
O, si. Muy bonita, he replied.
We didn't know he'd heard the words reserved

but for ourselves. His sweet response implied
no disrespect. He asked us if our food was good.
Mui bien. So patient as you tried

to speak in Spanish, and he understood
despite your faltering attempt. We knew
his name was Hector from his tag, but would

have known him anyway, just as we grew
to know Maria, who had made the bed
and swept the floor when we first came, but through

the years advanced to waitress. Hector said
her name aloud more often than the waves
had kissed the shore. We ate before you led

me to the sand. We walked atop the graves
of shellfish, seaweed, Mayan dreams, and held
each other's hand. Recalled the ruins, caves,

the birds, the manta rays we'd seen. Compelled
to never leave, we talked and touched and strolled
until the beach engulfed our feet. I smelled

Caribbean upon your skin. You told
me I was meant to have hibiscus in
my hair. Celestial hues turned azure gold,

with streaks of pinkish purple. Clouds as thin
as time illuminated heaven's grace.
Soft twilight sparkled brume. A silly grin

a permanent attachment to my face.
I fell in love with Mexico. I fell
in love with you again, inside a place

where Hector and Maria cast their spell
and made a million memories to tell.

I HATE THOSE IN-YOUR-FACE
SLAMMING POLITICAL PROTEST
POEMS ... OF 1999

This isn't a poem about politics,
social injustice or class distinction.
This isn't to point out the heretics
who grow obese from the earth's extinction.

This isn't about immigrants who die
in the desert before they arrive. No.
It's not about fat cats who never cry
for the working poor or the chronic, slow

decline of civil and human rights, right
here in a place where abortion is banned
because it's murder, as the moral white
have determined this the rule of the land.

In the same place where children are gunned down
on their doorsteps then stepped over because
they're black, or Mexican or worse. Who drown
in the blood of poverty, hate and laws.

It has nothing to do with killing fags,
because those who say sodomy is wrong
are the same ones who wear hoods and wave flags
and walk away and sing their marching song

while H-M-O's fuck you up the ass. Nope.
It's not about that. Not about blaming
the junky, punk-pusher peddling his dope
for the war on drugs, while white-lined, flaming

free-based, heroin shooting movie stars
are pampered by the press. Or prisons filled
with impoverished petty thieves, behind bars
for life, while wealthy rapists who have killed

for fun get plea bargains. Or the welfare
state held culpable for United States
economic downfall. For what's fair
about giving out handouts, when Bill Gates

Michael Eisner and Ted Turner had to
work for their fortunes? Well, that's what George Bush
preached while he was milking junk bonds from two
world forces so Michael Milken could push

R. J. Reynolds into that takeover.
Why it was pure entrepreneurial
genius, I heard it said, to makeover
a company to line their cereal

boxes with tobacco ads. *Buy two bags*
of cookies get one pack of cigarettes
free! They love their kids. Not like welfare hags,
who pop out kids only because it gets

them money. At least that's what George Bush says.
But this is not about that. Nor the crooked
cops who beat a man almost to death 'cause
he's Haitian, a criminal and wicked.

Not like New York City cops. Not about
buying Teddy Bears and little girl clothes
at discount prices from that super, stout,
mega discount department store that loathes

the likes of Howard Stern for he's lacking
decency. They can't rightfully sell his
merchandise because he's bad. But packing
stuff onto store shelves made in Taiwan is

good. Because it helps little eight-year-old
urchins who work fifteen hour days in
sweatshops buy food. Why two dollars is gold
to them. And it keeps them busy. We win.

They win. At least that's what the buyer at
Wal-Mart says. This isn't an anthem for
the AIDS boy, kicked out of school 'cause he sat
too close to the wholesome children with more

to live for. It's not about protecting
the free world by fighting to keep the oil
prices down. Or were those troops detecting
chemical warheads in order to spoil

the plans of a Middle Eastern madman?
Whatever. At least our soldiers came back
alive, all 700-hundred thousand. Can
you say that about Vietnam? No lack

of respect for these Veterans. Aching
joints, fatigue, memory loss. It's in their
heads. An illusion. There is no breaking
story in this Gulf War Syndrome crap. Where

could it come from? It's not the chemical
cocktail given to our bravest to keep
them healthy. Our leaders in medical
science proved that to be safe. What we reap

from blowing up aggressive nations is
insurmountable. So take your anthrax
like a good little war hero. This biz
ain't over yet. So sit back and relax.

It's not that. It's not about profiling,
redlining, cross-burning, segregating
schools, or ignorant skinheads reviling
Jews. It's not about the relegating

81

of workers for corporate gain, or of war
or white-collar crime or acid rain. No
message of a victimized woman or
of global disaster, nuclear snow

or violence or tyranny. That's not it!
Because I hate that self-serving, spoiled brat,
in-your-face slamming political shit
and I would never write a poem like that!

I CAN'T SING
couplets

I can't sing. Not a note worth hearing anyway.
I can't roll a melody, make the body sway.

I want to sing. I want to ring through air and walls
and time. But I can't bring a song that swings and falls

and rises in a rhyme. A blues-man cried the way
the sax-man blew a jagged heartbreak, soulful. *Play,*

he sighed. Desire became his fire and all the world
was his to own. But I can't sing the way he curled

the notes around his breath and swirled his sorrow down
the reed. I want to sing a song that's deepest brown

for you. But I can't find the song that rights the wrong,
that sails a sunrise to a brighter place along

horizons filled with grace. Oh, to erase a pain
with music and caress your skin with each refrain.

To love the lost through simple notes. To heal the heart
the way a ballad cries and shatters, breaks apart

the clinging hurt, eternal ache and chronic sting
that comes with living. No, forgive me, I can't sing.

So please forgive me, for the notes off-key can't set
you free, and the static stucco of the beat get

lost on me. Ripples rounding out expanding ride
the waves of water crashing when harmonics glide,

lift you from there, where your sitting. Take you out,
outside your body. Roam about your head and shout

out to the world that you are singing, even if
your mouth's not moving, even if your lips are stiff

even if your toes aren't tapping or your fingers
drumming. Still the music plays inside and lingers

in your soul. If I brought you in the song with me
then we'd escape reality and live so free.

Beyond the morning when the sun destroys the dream.
Into the afternoon when human spirits seem

to fall into the sidewalk cracks and tangle in
the weeds. That's when I want to bring you back, begin

the dream again. If I had a song to make you
strong, then you could hide it out of view in your shoe

or in an inside pocket. No one could take it,
break it, shake it loose from where it's hidden make it

something that it's not. It would only be a song
one that rights the wrong and sails the sunrise along

horizons filled with grace. Why it seems so easy
when I hear it come from somewhere in the trees. See

it in waves of heat along the blacktop highway.
Feel it in breezy air whistling in the archway.

Mingle in the cobwebs impossible to hide.
Taste it when the lemons zing and smell it inside

smoke. But I can't give you that, my love. I can't bring
to you or play for you, a song that I can't sing.

EPIPHANY
an English sonnet

I met Epiphany. I must attest
a quirky creature, winged, obscured in space.
I tried to catch it as it was to rest
directly on the nose upon my face.
With simple revelation, clear and bold,
it wrapped a cozy blanket 'round my head
and instantly relieved me from the cold.
Then whispered wisdom in my ear. It said,
I'm something other than you think, my dear.
I'm much too close for you to clearly see.
I can't be captured as a souvenir,
just witnessed for a moment, then let free.
I know not who it was or whence it came,
but surely I will never be the same.

Eileen Albrizio

is the Connecticut host for WNPR's news program *All Things Considered*, a broadcast journalist and National Public Radio newscast correspondent. She is also a promotional voice for PBS television. In addition to her full-time broadcasting career, Eileen is a playwright, freelance fine-art and portrait photographer, and visual arts director of The Buttonwood Tree, a nonprofit, multi-art venue in Connecticut.

She studied theatre at Central Connecticut State University, poetry at Asnuntuck College, photography at the Hartford Art School, playwriting at Wesleyan University, and broadcasting at the Connecticut School of Broadcasting. She is the recipient of several news awards, including the *1996 Best Newscast, 1998 Best Feature* and *2000 Best Spot News* awards from the Associated Press, as well as the *1999 Best Feature* and *1999 Best Spot News* awards from the Society of Professional Journalists. *Rain: Dark as Water in Winter*, follows her first book, *Messy on the Inside*, published in 1998. She has been published in numerous literary journals and was recognized several times by Writer's Digest for her plays and poetry. Eileen's plays, poetry and photography have been featured at various venues throughout the Northeast.

She and her husband, Wayne Horgan, co-own a comic book store in Rocky Hill, CT. They live happily together in the Hartford area with their three cats, Trouble, Buddy and Smoochee.